Making Things

by Marcia S. Freeman

ROURKE CLASSROOM RESOURCES

The path to student success

You can pedal a bike.

You can kick a soccer ball.

You can carry a bale of hay.

You can rake leaves.

You can lift grocery bags.

You can push and pull a pencil.

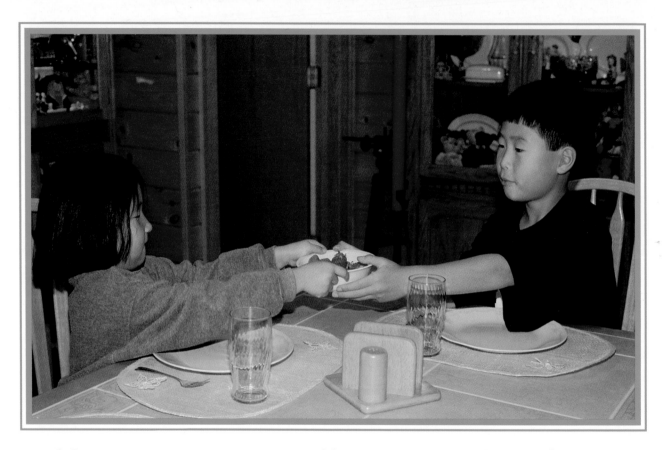

You can pass the strawberries.
Please!